Angel of the Prairie

Prairie

**The Heroic Story of Hazel Miner during the
North Dakota Blizzard of 1920**

Other books by Kevin Kremer:

A Kremer Christmas Miracle

Spaceship Over North Dakota

Saved by Custer's Ghost

The Blizzard of the Millennium

When it Snows in Sarasota

Santa's Our Substitute Teacher

Are You Smarter Than A Flying Gator

Maggie's Christmas Miracle

The Year Our Teacher Won the Super Bowl

The Most Amazing Halloween Ever

Are You Smarter Than A Flying Teddy

The Worst Day of School EVER – Do-Over

Valentine Shmellentine

Angel of the Prairie

The Heroic Story of Hazel Miner during the North Dakota Blizzard of 1920

by Kevin Kremer

Illustrated by Dave Ely

Published by Kremer Publishing
2019
P.O. Box 1385
Osprey, FL 34229-1385
KevinKremerBooks.com

Copyright © 2019 by Kevin Kremer
Second Edition

Kremer Publishing
P.O. Box 1385
Osprey, FL 34229-1385

Visit us on the Web! KevinKremerBooks.com

All rights reserved.

ISBN-13: 978-1-7333492-4-6

Without limiting the rights under copyright reserved above, no part of this publication may be reproduced, stored in or introduced into a retrieval system, or transmitted, in any form, or by any means (electronic, mechanical, photocopying, recording, or otherwise), without the prior written permission of both the copyright owner and the above publisher of this book.

*Special thanks to Penny Pulver,
Sharon Anderson, Jacky Schulte, Clay Starck,
Howard Bieber, Mikiel and Odell Ottmar,
and Duane Roth for all their help
with this project.*

*A special thanks to Drake Roush,
my grandnephew, for sparking my interest
in this amazing true story.*

**Sharon Anderson at Pioneer Days
in Center, North Dakota, 2014**

Hazel Miner

*Special thanks to Penny Pulver,
Sharon Anderson, Jacky Schulte, Clay Starck,
Howard Bieber, Mikiel and Odell Ottmar,
and Duane Roth for all their help
with this project.*

*A special thanks to Drake Roush,
my grandnephew, for sparking my interest
in this amazing true story.*

**Sharon Anderson at Pioneer Days
in Center, North Dakota, 2014**

Chapter 1

IT WAS A SNOWY, stormy Friday night in early March in Bismarck, North Dakota.

"Kinley! Thomas!" Mother called from the bottom of the stairs. "Your grandpa just pulled into the driveway in his truck!"

Eleven-year-old Kinley and her ten-year-old brother, Thomas, came running down the stairs, each with a duffle bag in hand. They both couldn't wait to spend the weekend with their grandpa in Mandan.

The two kids were met by their mom and dad at the bottom of the stairs. "Don't forget to take your snowmobile suits along," Father said. "I have a feeling you and your grandpa will be out playing in this weather."

"I can't wait!" Kinley said excitedly, as she and Thomas went to the closet near the front door.

Grandpa knocked and walked inside. At six feet, four inches, his head barely cleared the top of the doorway.

Grandpa was wearing a brown leather jacket, blue jeans, and his favorite Pittsburgh Steelers cap covering up most of his black and gray curly hair.

"Hi, everyone!" he said in his typical enthusiastic, friendly voice.

Kinley gave Grandpa a big hug. "Hi, Grandpa!"

Thomas took his turn hugging his grandpa. "Good to see you, Grandpa!"

Mother was next. "Hi, Dad! You're looking great!" she said, hugging and kissing him.

"How's it going, Mike?" said Father, shaking Grandpa's hand. "Are we going to get a big snowstorm out of this?"

"I've heard there will be lots of wet snow but not much wind," Grandpa replied. "The farmers should love it."

Grandpa looked at Kinley and Thomas and smiled. "This storm should give us perfect snow for building snowmen and snow forts in my backyard this weekend," he said.

"Excellent!" said Thomas. "Kinley and I have some great new ideas for snow forts."

"Yeah, Grandpa," Kinley added.

"Well, let's get going and get right on it then," said Grandpa. "Is there anything I can carry for you two?"

"No, Grandpa," said Thomas. "We both just have a duffle bag and our snowmobile suits."

"All right," Grandpa said, turning his attention to Mother and Father. "You two have fun in Minneapolis this weekend."

"We will," said Mother.

"We'll see you on Sunday," Father said. "Don't have too much fun, you three Musketeers."

"That's hard not to do with Grandpa," said Kinley, as she gave both her parents a good-bye hug and kiss.

"Don't forget to check that store in the Mall of America for Steelers stuff," said Thomas, as he hugged both his parents.

"We won't," said Mother.

Grandpa, Kinley, and Thomas hurried out the door and ran to Grandpa's truck, whose engine was running in the driveway. They all got into the toasty, warm cab, and Grandpa backed out of the driveway.

Kinley and Thomas loved the fact that they lived in Bismarck, and their grandpa lived only seven miles away, in Mandan. It was always a special treat when they got to spend a weekend at his house when their parents went out of town.

"Next stop—A&B Pizza!" Grandpa said as they rode down the snow-covered street. He chuckled and said, "And what are we ordering tonight?"

Grandpa asked the question, but he already knew what the answer was. They always ordered two pizzas. One was a large pizza, half sauerkraut and Canadian bacon and the other half, sausage and pepperoni. The other pizza was a small house special. When they were done eating as much as they wanted, there was almost always some pizza left to take home for the next day.

The heavy snow came down all the way to Mandan. Grandpa drove down Main Street, turned right on Sixth Avenue N.E., then went one block north until they got to A&B. Grandpa parked the truck, they got out, and ran to the door of the restaurant.

When they got inside, they were immediately greeted

by the manager, Wally Joersz. "Hi, Kinley and Thomas! Hi, Mike!" he said. "Nice to see you all again! I'll get your pitcher of root beer right away. Are you ordering the usual?"

"Yes, Wally," said Grandpa.

"I'll have them start making the pizzas right away," said Wally, with a friendly smile.

"Thanks," said Grandpa.

While they were waiting for their pizzas, Thomas said, "Grandpa, didn't that huge blizzard that happened when you were a kid take place in March?"

Thomas and Kinley loved listening to Grandpa's stories, even if they had heard some of them many times before.

"You have an excellent memory, Thomas," said Grandpa. "It was actually March 2, 3, and 4, way back in 1966."

"Please tell us about that again," said Kinley.

"Sure," said Grandpa, smiling. "Well, that blizzard was definitely the biggest one during my lifetime and one of the biggest in North Dakota history. I'll never forget it ... I was a newspaper boy here in Mandan and when the blizzard was finally over after three days, our house and many of the houses on my paper route were almost completely buried in snow. Many of my customers had dug tunnels to their front doors, and I had to walk through those tunnels to deliver the newspapers. People didn't have all those snow tractors and snow blowers back then to help them, either. We had to all dig out with shovels."

"Did you know that big blizzard was coming?" asked Thomas.

"As I recall, we had plenty of warning that a snow

Angel of the Prairie

storm was coming, but no one could have predicted how strong it would get or how long it would last. The whole thing started at about noon on Wednesday, March 2. By Friday night, North Dakota had gone through winds up to 100 miles per hour, with about three feet of snow. There were snow drifts as high as 40 feet in some places!"

"Forty feet!?" said Kinley, in disbelief.

"Yup," said Grandpa. "I actually keep a couple of my favorite photos of that blizzard on my phone now. I'll show you."

Grandpa turned on his phone and searched for the photos.

"This is the best one," he said. "This is a guy who worked with your great-grandpa with the telephone company. You'll notice he's standing on a snow drift that goes almost to the top of this 40-foot telephone pole."

"That's amazing!" said Kinley as she took a good look at the photo.

"That's unbelievable!" said Thomas.

"Were you scared at all during that blizzard, Grandpa?" Kinley asked.

"Mostly *excited*," answered Grandpa. "I remember how much fun it was to be out of school—and to watch everything, mostly from our picture window. Our family played some great games together like Monopoly and Crazy Eights. Mom even let us help her bake some cookies. Our dad played some of our favorite Christmas music. All of us kids even got to go out in the backyard and play with our dad during the blizzard for short periods of time."

"What was that like?" Thomas asked.

"We were dressed so well that it was lots of fun," said Grandpa. "Everything was covered but our eyes … and I still remember how much it hurt when the snow hit my eyes in all that wind, and how cold I got in just a few minutes even with all those clothes on."

"I wish you had pictures of you out in that blizzard," said Thomas.

"So do I," said Grandpa. "I'll tell you something. It sure wasn't much fun for the people who were trapped in their cars on the highways or lost their electricity or got lost in that storm."

"I can't even imagine that," said Kinley.

"Did your family run out of food during the storm?" Thomas wanted to know.

"That was another fun part of the storm for us," said Grandpa. "By the second day we were out of bread and milk and a few other things. My dad and my two older brothers and I hiked from our house down to our uncle's grocery store about a mile-and-a-half away. Our uncle had opened the store up for anyone in town who could make it there. I remember our dad tied us all together with a rope around our waists, and we kept close together as we walked. We also knew we could knock on doors along the way and go inside if we needed to, so we never felt in any danger. It was really fun, but I still remember not even being able to see my brothers next to me sometimes, it was that bad."

"How many people died during that blizzard?" asked Thomas.

"If I remember right, five people died in North Dakota. Three adults died from heart attacks from shoveling all that heavy snow. Two young girls died on their farms when they got lost in the storm just walking from their farm houses to their barns to tend to the animals."

"That's so sad," said Kinley.

Grandpa said, "As you can imagine, thousands of animals died on the prairie in North Dakota during that storm. There was no way to get them all to safety."

"That must have been an incredible experience, Grandpa," said Thomas. "Do you have a second-favorite blizzard story?"

"I sure do," Grandpa replied. "This is one I've never told you about. It happened way back in 1920, long before I was born. I've been doing some reading and research about it for quite a while now."

"Can you tell us about it?" Kinley asked.

Grandpa thought for a few seconds. "I'll tell you what," he said, "let's make some chocolate chip cookies when we get to my house, and I'll tell you about it after that. I've got some photos and stuff on my computer that will help me tell the story just the way I want to."

Kevin Kremer

"Warm chocolate chip cookies with a good blizzard story—it doesn't get any better than that!" said Thomas.

Chapter 2

AS SOON AS they got done eating at A&B Pizza, they headed for Grandpa's house on Sunset Drive in Mandan. When they got there, Kinley and Thomas immediately hung up their snowmobile suits and took their duffle bags to the rooms where they'd be sleeping.

Kinley liked to sleep in the guest room on the main floor. Thomas liked the family room downstairs, where he slept on the comfortable leather couch.

After dropping off their duffle bags, the two kids hurried to the kitchen. Grandpa was already getting everything organized so they could make his fantastic chocolate chip cookies.

"All right," Grandpa said, reaching into a cabinet for the vanilla, "you two need to wash up really good before we get started."

Kinley went over to the kitchen sink and said, "Grandpa, could you start telling us your other blizzard story while we're making cookies?"

"Let's get the cookies made first," Grandpa replied. "I

don't want us to make any mistakes with the ingredients or anything."

Kinley and Thomas finished washing their hands, then joined Grandpa by the kitchen counter. The electric mixer was there, along with the chocolate chip cookie recipe card and all the ingredients they would need.

"OK," said Grandpa. "Here we go. Thomas, you can turn the oven on to 375."

"Will do," said Thomas, walking over to the oven. "Done!" he said when he was finished.

"Very good," said Grandpa. "Now, I'll let you two measure the first ingredients and put them in the bowl."

"Butter first," said Kinley.

"That's right," said Grandpa. "We need two-thirds of a cup of butter, and that's about ten and two-thirds tablespoons on this butter stick." He handed the butter stick to Kinley. "I didn't have time to set it out, so you can cut the stick up into pieces and put them into the bowl."

Kinley went over to the small cutting board nearby and cut the butter stick up, then returned and pushed the pieces into the mixing bowl with the knife. Grandpa started the mixer at a low speed. After that, Kinley and Thomas took turns putting some more ingredients in the bowl. They were: two-thirds of a cup of shortening, one cup of granulated sugar, and one cup of brown sugar, packed.

"Excellent," said Grandpa when they'd finished. "Now we'll mix these together on high before we add anything else."

Kinley turned the mixer on high for a few minutes and they watched the ingredients mix up really well.

Angel of the Prairie

"Okay," said Grandpa, "now we're going to put two eggs and two teaspoons of vanilla in there."

Thomas put two teaspoons of vanilla in the bowl. Grandpa cracked the two eggs and added them to the other ingredients and they mixed everything up thoroughly on high.

After that was done, Grandpa said, "Now Kinley, you need to turn the mixer down to *low* before we add the baking soda, salt, and flour."

Kinley turned the mixer down to *low*.

"I'll put in the one teaspoon of baking soda and one teaspoon of salt," said Thomas, and he added them to the bowl.

"I'll do the three cups of Gold Medal flour," said Kinley, as she added them to the mixing bowl, one cup at a time.

After a few minutes, Grandpa said, "All right. Turn off the mixer, Kinley."

Kinley turned off the mixer. Grandpa touched the dough and said, "It seems a little sticky. Let's add another half cup of flour or so."

Thomas poured in another half cup of flour, and Grandpa checked the dough again.

"That's excellent," he said. "Now, let's add the package of semisweet chocolate chips."

"I'll take care of that," said Kinley, as she poured in the chocolate chips from the open bag nearby.

"Thomas," said Grandpa, "now you can mix them in there with the spatula."

Thomas mixed the chocolate chips into the dough. "That's excellent," Grandpa said when Thomas was done.

"Now, let's go over to the kitchen table. You two can put rounded balls of cookie dough, about two teaspoons full each, on the parchment paper I put on the cookie sheets. Put them about two inches apart."

Kinley and Thomas took their time putting the rounded balls of cookie dough on the cookie sheets.

"Grandpa," asked Thomas, "where did you get this recipe again?"

"Your great aunt Karol Volk gave it to me," he answered. "She's got the reputation for making the best chocolate chip cookies anywhere, and no one seems to be able to make them quite as good as she does."

"I can't believe she makes them any better than you, Grandpa," said Kinley. "They're the best!"

"Yeah, Grandpa," Thomas added.

"Well, thanks," said Grandpa with a big smile. "With all your help, I think these will be our best ever! Great Aunt Karol always says that the secret to her cookies is putting plenty of love into making them, and I think we're doing that."

"We sure are, Grandpa," said Thomas.

When Kinley and Thomas had finished putting all the rounded balls of cookie dough on the parchment paper, Grandpa said, "That's perfect! Now, Great Aunt Karol says the recipe calls for eight to ten minutes of baking, but I've found they usually take about ten to twelve minutes to bake. Set the timer for nine minutes, and we'll take a peek in the oven when it goes off."

Thomas put a pan of unbaked cookies in the oven.

Kinley asked, "Grandpa, was it even possible to make chocolate chip cookies back in 1920?"

Angel of the Prairie

Grandpa looked puzzled. "Thomas, go get my laptop computer in my office. Let's find out."

Thomas got the laptop and ran back and put it on the kitchen table. Grandpa turned it on, and said, "Kinley, I'll let you search for the answer."

"This is way too cool," said Kinley, when she had found it. "No chocolate chip cookies in 1920! It says chocolate chip cookies were invented in the 1930s by Ruth Wakefield at her Toll House restaurant in Whitman, Massachusetts. In 1939, Wakefield gave the Nestle Chocolate Company the right to use her recipe and the Toll House name.

"Did she get rich?" asked Thomas.

"Not even close," said Kinley. "It says here she was promised a dollar, which she told people she never even got. But it also says she got free chocolate for life, so that's not so bad."

"What made her think of putting chocolate chips in her dough that first time anyway?" Grandpa wanted to know.

"They don't seem to be sure exactly how it happened," Kinley said, "but many people think she was making cookies at her restaurant and she ran out of nuts. So she decided to chop up a semisweet chocolate bar she had received as a gift from Andrew Nestle from the Nestle Chocolate Company."

"That's pretty incredible," said Grandpa.

"Yeah," said Thomas. "Is that Toll House restaurant still around?"

"No," Kinley answered. "It burned down on New Year's Eve in 1984, and they never rebuilt it for some reason."

Toll House

"Grandpa," said Thomas, "can you even imagine how long it would have taken us to answer a question like this back in 1920 without a computer?"

"That's for sure," said Grandpa. "When I was a kid, our family had a group of books in our bookcase called the *World Book Encyclopedias* where we looked up a lot of things, but they were pretty limited compared to the Internet."

"Grandpa," said Thomas, with a chuckle, "with none of your chocolate chip cookies around and no Internet, I'm sure glad I wasn't alive back in 1920!"

"Me, neither," said Kinley, giggling.

Chapter 3

AFTER THEY FINISHED baking all the chocolate chip cookies, they sat around the kitchen table. Each of them had a warm cookie on a plate in front of them.

"Can we talk about that blizzard now?" Kinley asked.

"Sure," Grandpa replied. "Before we talk about the actual blizzard, though, let's turn the clock back about 100 years to 1920. Imagine living on a small farm about 32 miles north-northwest of here, near Center, North Dakota. Think about how different your life would be."

"We already know there were no chocolate chip cookies," said Thomas. "I'm guessing you and I wouldn't be watching Pittsburgh Steelers games together on Sundays either."

Grandpa giggled. "That would be correct, Thomas. If I recall, there were no television stations at all in North Dakota until about 1953. There weren't even any radio stations until 1922."

"Yikes!" said Thomas. "I'm not too thrilled about this life at all."

"Plus, there was no NFL until 1922," Grandpa added. "And the Steelers weren't around until 1933."

"It sounds like an *unbearably* tough life for you two guys so far," said Kinley.

"It really wasn't easy," said Grandpa. "But not just because of no NFL games on television and no chocolate chip cookies or Internet. Just imagine having to wash your clothes without an automatic washer and dryer. Imagine taking a bath when you had to heat the water one pot at a time. Imagine doing all the farm work without modern equipment and having no electricity at all."

"Did the people on our farm at least have a car?" Kinley wanted to know.

"I'm not sure, although there were definitely cars around by this time," Grandpa replied. "The blizzard story I'm going to tell you about took place in March. There was still some snow on the ground, and the kids in the story actually took a horse-drawn sleigh back and forth to school."

"That's something I would like," said Kinley. "That would be fun."

"I think so, too," said Grandpa. "There was a barn close to the school, so students could keep the horses in there. The older kids could tend to the horses during recess and noon hour."

"I'll bet their school was a lot different than ours," said Thomas.

"No doubt," said Grandpa. "You've seen some of the old *Little House on the Prairie* episodes on TV. The school in this story was called the Center Consolidated School, and it was a lot like that, with no electricity, not very good heat in the winter, and those great black chalkboards. The school had two rooms with a teacher for the younger kids and a teacher for the older ones. There were about 35 kids in the school, covering the first eight grades, with kids all the way up to age 17. There was a little place near the school, not much bigger than my shed, called the *Teacherage*. That's where the two teachers stayed."

Center Consolidated School in 1950

"How did you find out all that stuff about the school, Grandpa?" asked Thomas.

"I called some people in Center who knew about it," Grandpa answered.

"Do you know if it's still there?" asked Kinley.

"They told me it was," Grandpa replied. "It's there, but it has been remodeled. It's a house now. The school barn is still around too, but it was moved somewhere nearby."

"Too cool," said Thomas.

"Grandpa," said Kinley, "let's say that right now, you had to go back and live in the year 1920. What modern thing do you think you'd miss the most?"

"Kinley, that's a great question," said Grandpa. "Let me think ... my grandparents actually lived on a farm near Linton, North Dakota, at about that time. From talking to them, I'd have to say what I'd miss most would be indoor plumbing. Before they had indoor plumbing and running water and all that, they had to go outdoors and use the outhouse when they needed to go to the bathroom. As you know from some of our camping in Canada, outhouses weren't much more than tiny wooden houses built over a hole in the ground with a wooden seat built over it. Imagine having to go out there in the middle of the winter."

"I don't even want to think about that!" Thomas exclaimed, with a weird look on his face.

"Grandpa?" said Kinley. "Could we please change the subject before you totally gross me out?"

"Sure," said Grandpa, chuckling.

"Let me ask you another question," said Kinley. "What would you have liked the *most* about living on a farm in North Dakota back in 1920?"

Angel of the Prairie

"That's easy," said Grandpa. "In the story I'll be telling you, you can tell how close neighbors were back then. They all knew each other and pitched together to help each other out. I think people were closer than they are now. Today people have all the fancy gadgets to communicate, but they don't even know their next door neighbors."

Grandpa's ring tone sounded. He looked down at his phone. "I just got a text from your parents. Their plane is just about ready to take off for Minneapolis."

"Hey, Grandpa," said Thomas. "You didn't mention telephones. Did they have telephones on this farm and school in this blizzard story you're going to tell us about?"

"I'm glad you asked," said Grandpa, "because that actually plays a pretty important part in the story. Many of the farms I'll be telling you about had telephones, and the school did too ... but nothing like the fancy phones everyone carries around now. Thomas, would you please go get my marker board downstairs so I can do a better job trying to explain some of this?"

"Sure, Grandpa," replied Thomas.

Chapter 4

"THESE COOKIES ARE the best!" said Kinley, as she enjoyed another hot chocolate chip cookie with milk.

"Great Aunt Karol would be proud of us," said Thomas, taking a bite of his cookie.

"She would be very proud of you two," said Grandpa, finishing his cookie. "You did a great job! Now, you two can just keep eating, and I'll try to explain the telephone system back on the farms in the Center area in 1920."

Grandpa stood up and started drawing on his marker board. "So," he began, "imagine we had a bunch of farms. Let's just say there were about 20. I'm just going to draw a few of them. Now, imagine all the farms are connected by a pair of copper wires in a long cable on telephone poles that carry all the calls that people make. The cable runs from pole to pole and from farm to farm, and it connects to a phone on each farm. Eventually the telephone cable runs into the town of Center, where an operator sits. She takes care of any calls that need go outside of our farms here."

Angel of the Prairie

"You draw good illustrations," said Thomas.

"Yeah, Grandpa," said Kinley.

"Thanks, but you two are much too kind," said Grandpa, chuckling. "Now, I've got to show you what the

phones looked like back then, but I'm not going to try to draw one. I'll find a good photo for you on my computer."

Grandpa found a photo of an old phone and made it as large as he could on his computer screen. "I'll keep this on the computer to refer to as we go," he said.

Thomas laughed when he saw the photo of the phone on Grandpa's computer. "Compare that to the phones we have today, Grandpa," he said.

"A huge change in 100 years," said Kinley.

"That's for sure," said Grandpa. "So, anyway, many farms back then had a phone like this, and then we've got these farms connected by this telephone cable that carries all the phone calls. Now, here's the part that's hard to imagine. All the farms actually shared the same telephone line. It was called a Party Line."

Kinley had a look of surprise on her face. "You don't mean everyone could listen in to everyone else's calls on this Party Line, do you?" she asked.

"Well, yes," Grandpa replied, "but they really weren't supposed to be doing that. There wasn't supposed to be one big party on the Party Line," he said with a chuckle. "Let me try to explain how it was supposed to work."

Grandpa pointed to the receiver on the left side of the picture of the phone on his computer screen. "OK," said Grandpa, "let's say you wanted to talk to your friend Katrice, who lives on a farm on this same Party Line. First, to find out if it was okay to call, you'd carefully lift up the receiver from the hook on the left over here, put it up to your ear, and listen. If you didn't hear anyone talking, then you would have to put your mouth really close to this transmitter piece here in the middle and speak loudly and clearly and say 'Using?'—

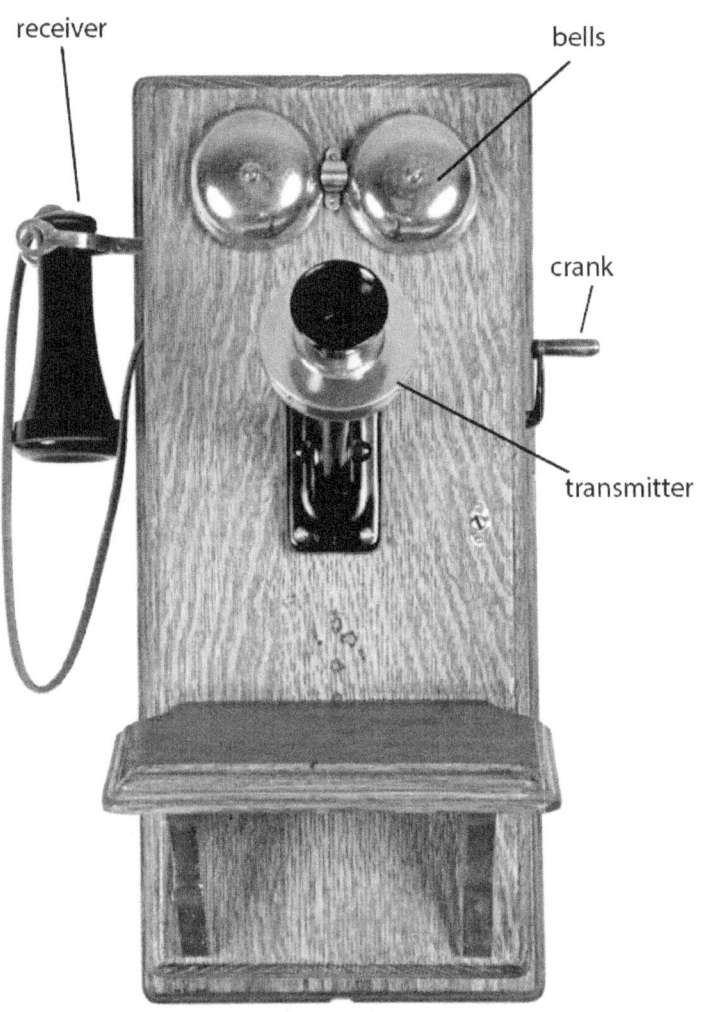

which was a way to ask 'Is anyone using the line?' If there was no answer, then you could make your call. But if someone was using the line, then the most courteous thing to do would be to hang up and wait … but my parents and grandparents told me many people would carefully lift the receiver and listen in."

"It would have been tempting," said Thomas.

"You bet," said Grandpa. "It must have been agreat form of entertainment for them back then."

"Another reason why they needed football on TV," said Thomas, giggling.

"You're right," said Grandpa.

"Okay, let's say the line was free," said Kinley. "How could I call Katrice if there's no place to dial a number on the phone?" "Well," said Grandpa, "everyone in the party had a unique ring, based on long rings and short rings which you could make by turning the crank on the right side of the phone here which would then ring all the bells on the phones in the Party Line. Each farm house had a list of everyone else's calling signal near their phone. So, let's say you were calling Katrice and her call signal was one long ring and two short rings … to call her, you would make the long ring by turning the crank for about two seconds, then you would pause about a second. After that, to make the two short rings, you'd turn the crank one second, pause about a second, then turn the crank for one second again. Follow me so far?"

"Yes, I like this," said Thomas.

"Me too," said Kinley.

"Good," said Grandpa. "Now, if anyone was home at Katrice's, they would recognize their signal, pick up the

Angel of the Prairie

phone, and you'd ask for Katrice. When she got to the phone, she would have to speak really loud and clear into that transmitter there so you could hear her on the other end, so there wasn't much privacy in the house when anyone made a call. The connections and equipment weren't nearly as good as they are now."

Kinley summarized. "So, I'm talking to Katrice, and everyone in her house knows what we're saying because she's practically yelling, and the same goes in my house? Plus, a bunch of people on the Party Line are probably listening in, even if they're not supposed to."

"That's pretty much how it went," said Grandpa. "And when you were done with your call and had hung up, you'd give one short turn of the crank, producing one little tinkle on the bells, and that signaled to everyone on the Party Line that you were done with the call and the line was free again."

"Unreal," said Thomas. "What if we wanted to talk to someone in another town or someone not on our Party Line?"

Grandpa said, "That's when you have to call that operator I drew over here on the marker board. She could connect us to other telephone lines."

"That's pretty cool," said Kinley. "But why couldn't these people have their own private lines?"

"That service wasn't available yet to rural a reasin our country," said Grandpa. "Oh, there's actually one other feature that comes into this blizzard story I'm going to tell you. Let's say there's an emergency of some sort, and you want everyone on the Party Line to know about it. You'd hang up and turn the little crank vigorously so everyone would hear one long ring. This signaled that everyone on the Party Line should make a dash to the phone—and find out what happened."

"No need to text everyone," Thomas noted.

"That's right," said Grandpa.

Chapter 5

KINLEY GAVE GRANDPA a mischievous look and grinned. "Grandpa, are we *ever* going to get to that 1920 blizzard story?"

"Yes," Grandpa replied, chuckling. "I just thought we needed to cover a little background first."

"You know I'm just kidding, Grandpa," said Kinley. "I love the way you tell your stories."

"I knew you were just kidding," said Grandpa. "But, let me *really* start the story now. ... So, you two both know what it's like when we finally get those first couple of nice days in March after our long winters in North Dakota, right?"

"Everyone gets spring fever," said Kinley.

"You start seeing people wearing shorts and T-shirts, and it's only about 40 degrees outside," Thomas added. "For some reason, it almost feels hot."

"That's right," said Grandpa, "and some of my friends

start riding their motorcycles. Well, this story starts on one of those first nice days after a long winter—March 12, 1920. It was a Friday. The North Dakota people back then were definitely happy to finally get some good weather. A 19-year-old cowboy by the name of Rufus Cone was living on a ranch near Beulah, North Dakota, with his parents ... and Rufus *definitely* had spring fever."

"I've never heard the name Rufus before," said Kinley, chuckling.

"Yeah, Grandpa," said Thomas. "Rufus sounds like a good name for a *dog*."

Grandpa giggled. "As you know, popular names change over time," he said. "Did you know you had great-great-grandpas named Valentine and Alfonse? You had great-great-grandmas named Matilda and Ethyl. When's the last time you met someone with those names?"

"Never," said Kinley.

"Anyway," Grandpa said, "I've got a photo I found of Rufus when I was doing my research."

Grandpa quickly found the photo on his computer and showed it to his grandchildren.

"He was a real cowboy," said Thomas.

"Yes," said Grandpa, "Rufus was definitely a cowboy through and through. And with the nice weather they were having, Rufus felt like getting out and going for a long ride to visit some of his old friends near Center. You see, not too long before this, Rufus and his family had moved to the Beulah area from a farm near Center, North Dakota."
"How far is Center from Beulah?" asked Thomas.

"Center is about 25 miles southeast of Beulah," Grandpa answered. "Oh, I should also mention one other thing. Rufus was about to turn 20 the next Tuesday, on March 16, so I'm pretty sure he had that birthday on his mind."

"Grandpa, that's *your* birthday!" Kinley exclaimed.

"I think that's one of the reasons I like Rufus … and this whole story," said Grandpa. "So, anyway, since things weren't too busy at their ranch, Rufus's parents gave him the okay to visit his friends near Center. He got on the phone and called his friend, Orin Cook, who lived on a farm east of Center. Orin told Rufus that he had a place for him to sleep for as long as he wanted to stay. Rufus left early that Friday morning, and it took him most of the day to ride from Beulah to the Cooks' house.

"Rufus had a great time along the way. The sun was nice and warm. The North Dakota prairie was starting to thaw out. The blue sky over the open prairie was spectacular. Meadowlarks were singing. The signs of spring were everywhere.

"Now, on that same Friday morning, at the Blanche and William Miner Farm about five miles east of Center, three Miner children were getting ready for school. Hazel was 15, Emmet was 11, and Myrdith was almost nine."

"How far was the Miner farm from the Cook farm?" Thomas asked.

"The Miners lived about three miles north and a mile or so east of the Cooks," Grandpa answered. "I'll draw a little map of all of this later."

"Were there any other kids in the Miner family?" Kinley wanted to know.

"Yes," Grandpa replied. "Zelda was about 20 and Howard was about 5, but they didn't go to school. Oh, I actually have photos of the Miner kids and their parents on my computer."

"These are awesome!" said Kinley.

"Yeah, how did you get these?" asked Thomas.

"From a nice lady in Center who's been helping me with my research," Grandpa replied.

"Cool," said Kinley.

"I think photos and illustrations always add to a story

Angel of the Prairie

like this," said Grandpa. "Now, continuing the story … shortly after sunrise on this Friday, William hooked up their little jumper sleigh to the children's mare, named Maude. Then Hazel, Emmet, and Myrdith took their sleigh ride to school, just two miles south of their farm.

Emmet, Hazel, Howard, Zelda, and Myrdith

Mrs. Miner, Howard, and Mr. Miner

"So, while Rufus Cone was riding his horse to the Cooks' farm that Friday, the three Miner children were in school. As you can imagine, the fact that it was Friday and it was so nice outside, it must have been pretty difficult for anyone to concentrate on their lessons. Knowing this, I'll bet the teachers gave the kids a couple of long recesses."

"What kinds of things did they do at recess time back then?" Thomas asked.

"I did some research on that," said Grandpa, "and I found out that they played many of the games my friends and I used to play during recess at my elementary school in Mandan. I've told you about most of them before—games like marbles, jumping rope, red light-green light, captain may I, fox and geese, pom pom pull away, hop scotch, and red rover. There's one game they played at the Miners' school that I haven't told you about before that was lots of fun. We used to play it at our house."

"What was it?" asked Thomas.

"It was called *Ante I Over* or sometimes *Annie Annie Over*," said Grandpa. "You probably had to go to a much smaller school than the ones we attended to play this game."

"How did it work?" asked Kinley.

"We played with any kind of ball, but I think it would be the most fun with a soft playground ball. The kids got into two equal groups, one on each side of the school. Each group had an umpire to check on the other team. Then the ball is thrown over the school by any member of one group who says, 'Ante I Over!' The team on the other side watches the ball come over the roof, and tries to catch it. If the ball doesn't make it over and it rolls back to the same side as it was thrown, the group yells, 'Pig Tail!' Then they throw the ball again. If the ball is caught when it's thrown over to the other side, then the group catching it runs to the other side. The player with the ball tries to tag members of the other group with the ball as they run to the other side of the school. Since the ball wasn't too hard, we used to throw it at the members of the other team. If anyone gets tagged with the ball, he becomes a member of the group that caught him. When the recess is over, the group with the most members wins."

"That's so cool," said Kinley. "Can we play it sometime?"

"Sure," said Grandpa. "When the weather gets nicer, we'll invite some people from the neighborhood over. I'll bet it will bring back some great memories for some of the older folks."

"I can't wait," said Kinley.

"Grandpa, do you know if the Miner kids were good students?" Thomas asked.

"I think so," Grandpa replied. "Hazel was making plans to go to Bismarck High School the next fall."

"That's a long way to go to school each day," said Thomas.

"More than 35 miles," said Grandpa. "She would have had to stay with someone in Bismarck during the week and come home on weekends. I read that Hazel definitely had all the qualities you'd want in a good teacher. She loved children, she was responsible, and she had a sunny, cheerful disposition. Other kids liked Hazel a lot. They found her to be helpful and sympathetic."

"Do Rufus and the Miner kids ever meet in this story?" Thomas asked.

"They sure do," said Grandpa. "I'll get to that part of the story eventually."

Chapter 6

"WELL," SAID GRANDPA, "that weekend was absolutely terrific on the North Dakota prairie. With temperatures up as high as the mid-40s, much of the remaining snow disappeared. Some of the creeks started running again. The sun, the warm temperatures, and all the other signs of spring lifted everyone's spirits. And Rufus Cone had a great time riding his horse to nearby farms, visiting many of his friends."

"Did he ever visit the Miners?" asked Kinley.

"He sure did," Grandpa answered. "Rufus had actually gone to school with Zelda and Hazel, and they were friends, so he stopped by the Miners' place for an hour or so on Saturday afternoon. They had a great time reminiscing about some of their favorite times when they were going to school together, and they talked about their plans for the future. Hazel and Zelda had actually been invited to a surprise birthday partyfor Rufus at the Cooks' place the next Tuesday after school. Luckily, the two Miner girls did a good job not spilling the beans to Rufus about that party when they were talking."

"So the Cooks must have known about Rufus's birthday on March 16 even though he hadn't told them about it," said Kinley.

"That's right," said Grandpa. "I'll bet the Cooks remembered Rufus's birthday from past years, when he lived near Center."

Thomas cringed. "Grandpa, I'm getting the feeling there's a blizzard coming pretty soon, and no one knows it's coming."

"Me too," said Kinley. "They sure could have used the Weather Channel back then."

"That's for sure," said Grandpa, with a chuckle. "Actually, the weather began changing on Sunday evening. First, it started raining, and it rained pretty hard all through the night as the temperatures continued falling. At about midnight, the rain stopped, and soon it was snowing those big, beautiful snowflakes we often get at springtime. By the time William and Blanche Miner got out of bed at 4:30 a.m., the view from their window was like the inside of a beautiful snow globe. Massive numbers of those huge snowflakes were coming down in a light breeze.

"Mr. and Mrs. Miner were up having an early morning cup of coffee, and they were looking out the window, talking about how beautiful it was outside. While they were talking, Mrs. Miner asked her husband if he thought a blizzard was coming. He told her that he didn't think so, but they needed to watch the conditions carefully. If things got worse after the kids got to school, William said he would ride his horse to the school and get the kids.

"Meanwhile, over at the Cook farm, Rufus was sitting by the fire. He was enjoying his coffee and looking out the window, watching the weather. He wasn't heading back to Beulah until Wednesday or Thursday anyway, so he wasn't concerned about the weather at all. Besides, he knew all the moisture at this time of the year would be good for all the farmers.

"Later, as all the Miners were around the table eating breakfast, William told Hazel, 'The conditions don't seem too bad right now. It's about 15 degrees. I'll hitch Maude to the jumper, and you should be fine going to school. If the weather gets bad, I'll ride to school, and I'll tie my horse to the back of the sleigh. Then we can go home together.'

"Hazel said, 'That's good, Daddy. We will be just fine.'

"Then little Myrdith said, 'I like stormy days in school. Our teacher lets us play fun games inside during recess.'

"Emmet wasn't quite as thrilled about the idea of a snow storm. He said, 'I hope the snow stops. I want spring to be here for good.'

"As the jumper sled left the farm for school that morning, Blanche said to William, 'I have a bad feeling about this weather.'

"'Don't worry,' William said to his wife, 'with Maude and Hazel in charge, the kids will be fine getting to school. If this weather does turn into a storm, I'll go get them.'"

Chapter 7

KINLEY HAD A worried look on her face. "Grandpa, did they make it to school okay?"

"Yes, they did," Grandpa replied. "It was snowing really hard, but the wind wasn't too bad. It wasn't that cold either, in the mid-teens. When they got to school, Emmet unhitched Maude next to the barn, as Hazel and Myrdith ran into the school, holding hands. The jumper sled was left on the side of the barn, out of the wind, and Emmet took Maude into the barn where there were already several other horses and mules.

"After school started, the weather just got worse and worse. The temperature dropped and the winds picked up big-time. By morning recess time, the visibility was pretty bad and everyone knew they had a winter storm on their hands."

"Was everyone stuck in the school?" asked Thomas.

"Well," said Grandpa, "they sure didn't go outside for

morning recess, although some of the older boys ran out to the barn to tend the horses and mules. The kids back in the classroom played a game called *I Spy*."

"How does that work, Grandpa?" Kinley wanted to know. "It's a pretty simple game where an item was hidden around the room by the teacher, something small or large, maybe a little ball or a mitten or something. Then the children would quietly go around the room and try to be the first to find it. The first person to find it tried not to give away the location to the others, but he or she would call out the words ***I Spy!***—and then sit down. The other kids would keep trying to find it and they would also try not to give away the location. They would also say the words ***I Spy***—and then sit down. After a certain amount of time, when almost everyone had found the object, the first person who said ***I Spy*** would get to tell where it was and hide something else."

"That's a cool game," said Thomas. "I'm going to tell my teacher about it."

"Me too," said Kinley. "Maybe we can play it sometime this weekend, Grandpa."

"Sure," said Grandpa. "It would probably be more fun with a bunch of people, but we won't let that stop us."

"Grandpa," said Thomas, "I'll bet the weather got worse after recess, didn't it?"

"It sure did. The winds picked up, the visibility got worse and worse, and before noon, there were full-fledged blizzard conditions."

"Did they cancel school after that?" asked Kinley.

"They had a blizzard rule," Grandpa explained. "No one could leave school until a parent either picked them up personally or called the school on the Party Line and said their children could go home on their own. William Miner took off for the school at about noon to pick up Hazel, Myrdith, and Emmet, just like they talked about during breakfast."

"What was Rufus doing?" asked Kinley.

"Rufus and the Cooks were actually enjoying the view from inside their house," said Grandpa. "After all, the animals were all safe, and it was always fun watching a good storm, as long as you didn't have to be out in it. And Rufus was actually thinking about turning 20 the next day, but he didn't mention his birthday to Orin or his wife because he didn't want them to make a big deal about it."

"But they knew," said Kinley, smiling.

"They sure did," said Grandpa. "And back at the school, sleighs and bobsleds arrived, and parents picked up their kids. While the Miner kids and others waited, the teachers let them play some board games and some flash card games as long as they kept their voices down. They also watched the weather outside as it continued to get worse.

"William Miner's ride to school wasn't too bad with the wind at his back. He was dressed in all his warmest clothes. Mr. Miner had also brought some extra scarves and blankets for his three kids. When he got to the school, he put his horse in the school barn, then ran over to the school and opened the front door.

"'Hi, Daddy!' Myrdith said when she spotted William coming in the front door.

"William told them, 'I brought some extra scarves and blankets. Now, I'm going to go out and hitch Maude to the jumper. I'll be right back. Hazel, make sure everyone is bundled up good.'

"So, William ran out to the barn and got Maude and hooked her up to the sleigh, which was parked on the side of the barn out of the worst wind. Then he rode the sleigh to the front of the school and parked it by the front door. After that, he ran into the school to get his kids. He carried Myrdith out all bundled up, and Emmet and Hazel followed right behind them. William made sure the children were all cozy in the sleigh, with the blankets tucked around them. He told his three children, 'Now you stay covered up while I go get my horse out of the barn. I will tie him behind the jumper and drive you home.

"William ran to the barn and got his horse, but when he got back to the front of the school, the sleigh was gone!

"'Dang that mare!' William exclaimed. 'She must have taken off for home!'

"William quickly got on his horse and took off!"

Chapter 8

"WILLIAM MINER MUST have been frantic at this point," said Grandpa. "He took off for home, hoping and praying he would catch up with his kids somewhere along the way. Unfortunately, he didn't find them. He got home, hoping the kids would already be there, but they weren't."

"What did he do after that?" asked Kinley anxiously.

"He told Blanche he was headed back to the school. He wanted to retrace his steps, hoping he would find his three children this time. William went back out in that horrendous weather. He was only able to see a few feet in front of him most of the time, getting pelted by the wind-driven snow, hoping he would find the sleigh and his kids this time … but he didn't. Then he went back home and admitted to his wife … three of their kids were lost in the blizzard."

"I can't even *imagine* how they both must have felt," said Kinley.

"Me, neither," said Thomas.

"It must have been absolutely agonizing for both of them," said Grandpa. "At the Cooks, Mrs. Cook was preparing the evening meal. Rufus and Orin were sitting over by the fireplace talking. Suddenly, the Party Line emergency signal we talked about earlier was sounded."

"Those long rings?" said Thomas.

"That's right," said Grandpa. "Orin went over and picked up the receiver and listened, but he didn't say a word. By the look on his face, though, Rufus and Mrs. Cook could tell the news wasn't good. Finally, Orin turned and looked at Rufus and his wife and said, 'The Miner children are lost in their jumper in the blizzard!'

"Rufus looked out the window at the miserable conditions, and his heart dropped into his stomach. He knew how dangerous it was to spend even a few minutes out in a blizzard like this one. He couldn't even imagine being caught out in weather like this for hours—and *in the dark*.

"Orin's wife wanted to know how it had happened, so Orin explained to her, 'Bill Miner rode his horse to the school to pick up his kids. Then he hooked Maude up to the jumper, parked it in front of the school, and helped get the kids in the sleigh. Then he ran to get his horse from the school barn to tie to the back of the jumper so he could drive it home. When Bill got back from the barn, though, the jumper was gone.'

"'Is anyone going out searching in this awful weather tonight?' Mrs. Cook asked Orin.

"'Some search parties are going out tonight, but that seems crazy in the dark,' Orin replied, looking out the window. 'Someone else is likely to get lost out in this blizzard.'

"Mrs. Cook said, 'We can pray that the Miner children

somehow find a place out of this wind tonight—and we will see where things stand in the morning.'

"Later that night," Grandpa continued, "more emergency phone calls revealed that a few search parties had tried to go out in the blizzard in the dark, but they soon found out that it was much too dangerous. Late that night, before they went to bed, Orin got on the phone and started organizing a search party. They tentatively decided that if the three children weren't found during the night, everyone who could make it through the blizzard would meet at the school in the morning."party. They tentatively decided that if the three children weren't found during the night, everyone who could make it through the blizzard would meet at the school in the morning."

Chapter 9

"WHAT HAPPENED TO the sleigh, Grandpa?" Kinley asked, looking very worried.

"I think I'm going to need my marker board for this part of the story," said Grandpa. "Would you please erase it for me, Thomas?"

"Sure," said Thomas, as he picked up the eraser and began erasing.

"So ... picture this," said Grandpa, drawing on the marker board, "we've got Center Consolidated School here with a barn nearby. Then there's a fence around the school, and there's a north gate and a south gate you pass through to get on and off the school grounds. The Miners lived about two miles north of the school. The Cooks lived just over a mile southwest of the school. The town of Center is about five miles west of the school. The other thing you need to know is ... there's a coulee that runs something like this between the Miners and the school."

Grandpa drew the coulee and then stopped.

"What's a coulee?" Kinley wanted to know.

"It's like a small valley," Grandpa answered. "I'll bet you can find a photo of a coulee on the Internet quicker than I can."

Coulee

It took Kinley only about 15 seconds to find a photo of a coulee.

"That's perfect," said Grandpa. "Down at the bottom of the coulee, you might have a stream flowing at least part of the year. I've heard the words *ravine* or *gully* used to describe the same thing."

"I like the word *coulee* the best," said Thomas. "Me too," said Kinley.

"I do too," said Grandpa. "Now," he continued, "the kids were out in front of the school in the sleigh all bundled up. Their dad was going to the barn nearby to get his horse. Remember, William planned on tying his horse to the back of the sleigh for their trip back home. Th e weather was awful. Poor Maude was getting pelted in the face by snow, driven by wind gusts greater than 40 miles per hour."

"Maude takes off, trying to get out of the wind, doesn't she?" Thomas guessed.

"That's right," said Grandpa. "It turns out Maude was an incredible, tame horse, always very reliable. But she had spent much of the winter out on the range, and her natural instinct was to get her tail to the wind and her face out of those strong north winds pelting her with all that snow. When William Miner ran into the barn to get his horse, Maude turned her tail to the wind and pulled the sleigh out of the south gate. Usually, they would go out the north gate to get home. Before Hazel and the other kids knew what had happened, they were out in the middle of a blizzard. They were lost."

"That must have been awful," said Kinley.

"Hard to even imagine," said Grandpa. "They were out on the open prairie, with no real way to get their bearings because they couldn't see more than a few feet in any direction. To make matters even worse, the canvas cover of their sleigh had been ripped earlier by some of the horses when it had been left by their barn at home. Now, the wind started ripping the canvas cover more and more as time went on, so the three Miner children must have been getting really cold."

"And really scared, I'll bet," said Kinley.

"That's for sure," said Grandpa. "Now, I'm going to expand my map so you can get an idea of what happened to the sleigh after it went out the wrong gate. I'm going to put a **Number 1** here where Maude pulls the sleigh out the south gate. Once they got out of the gate some distance and they realized what had happened, Hazel was eventually able to grab the reins and turn Maude north. But right here, where I'm going to put a **Number 2**, something really bad happens."

"How could it get any worse?" Thomas asked.

"It does," said Grandpa. "They went over a ridge, down into this coulee. Once they got down in there, they had a big problem. You see, the coulee actually had water flowing in it during the warmer weather they were having, but now it was mainly heavy slush. The sleigh got stuck in it. The tugs came loose and Hazel had to get out of the sleigh to reconnect the tugs to Maude."

"What are tugs?" asked Thomas.

"They were basically leather straps with buckles that connected Maude to the sleigh," Grandpa answered. "So, Hazel gets out in her overshoes to reconnect those tugs. While she does that, she ends up in slush and water up to her waist. Now Hazel's soaked from the waist on down, and her overshoes are full of water. She leads Maude out of the coulee in those awful blizzard conditions."

"Poor Hazel!" Kinley exclaimed. "She must have been *freezing*."

"There's no doubt about that," said Grandpa. "It's sad, too, because they were actually only about 200 feet from the Wilson Farm house at this point, but they had no idea, because the blizzard was so bad. But Hazel acted with real determination and courage. Emmet was helpful too. The two of them took turns leading Maude through the blizzard after this, but unfortunately, they had no clue where they were. Maude was pretty incredible the whole time too. She just kept going. Once in a while Hazel or Emmet had to break the crust that formed around Maude's head from all the snow plus all the moisture coming out of Maude's mouth and nostrils."

Grandpa looked at Kinley and Thomas, who were totally spellbound by the story.

"After that mishap in the coulee," Grandpa continued, "they drifted east … then southeast … then east again. Right here where I'm putting a **Number 3**, they actually spotted a gate and it gave them some hope. They attempted to turn through that gate, but unfortunately, it was blocked by a big snow drift.

"How far were they from the school at this point?" Thomas wanted to know.

"Less than two miles, but it might as well have been 100 miles," said Grandpa. "They were lost out on the open prairie in weather conditions that were just *unbearable*. From there, they headed mostly south. Right here, where I'm putting a **Number 4**, it just got worse for them. They tipped over when the sleigh hit a steep slope going down into the coulee. Hazel was thrown over the dashboard of the sleigh into the snow. Then Emmet and Hazel tried to get the sleigh upright again, but they couldn't do it. To make matters even worse, it was getting dark."

Chapter 10

"TALK ABOUT A tough situation," said Grandpa. "Now they were lost in the blizzard, and their sleigh was tipped over on its side. It was pretty much jammed into some deep snow and slush."

"Now what, Grandpa?" Thomas asked, looking worried.

"Hazel knew she had to stay as upbeat as possible," Grandpa replied. "And first, they had to make the best shelter they could out of the overturned sleigh. I think I can draw what their shelter might have looked like based on what I've read."

"I'll erase the marker board again," Thomas offered.

"Thanks, Thomas," said Grandpa.

As soon as Thomas was done, Grandpa began drawing the overturned sleigh as he was talking. Grandpa said, "Hazel acted so courageously despite the fact that things just seemed to be getting worse and worse. The tipped-over sleigh provided some protection from the blizzard, but it

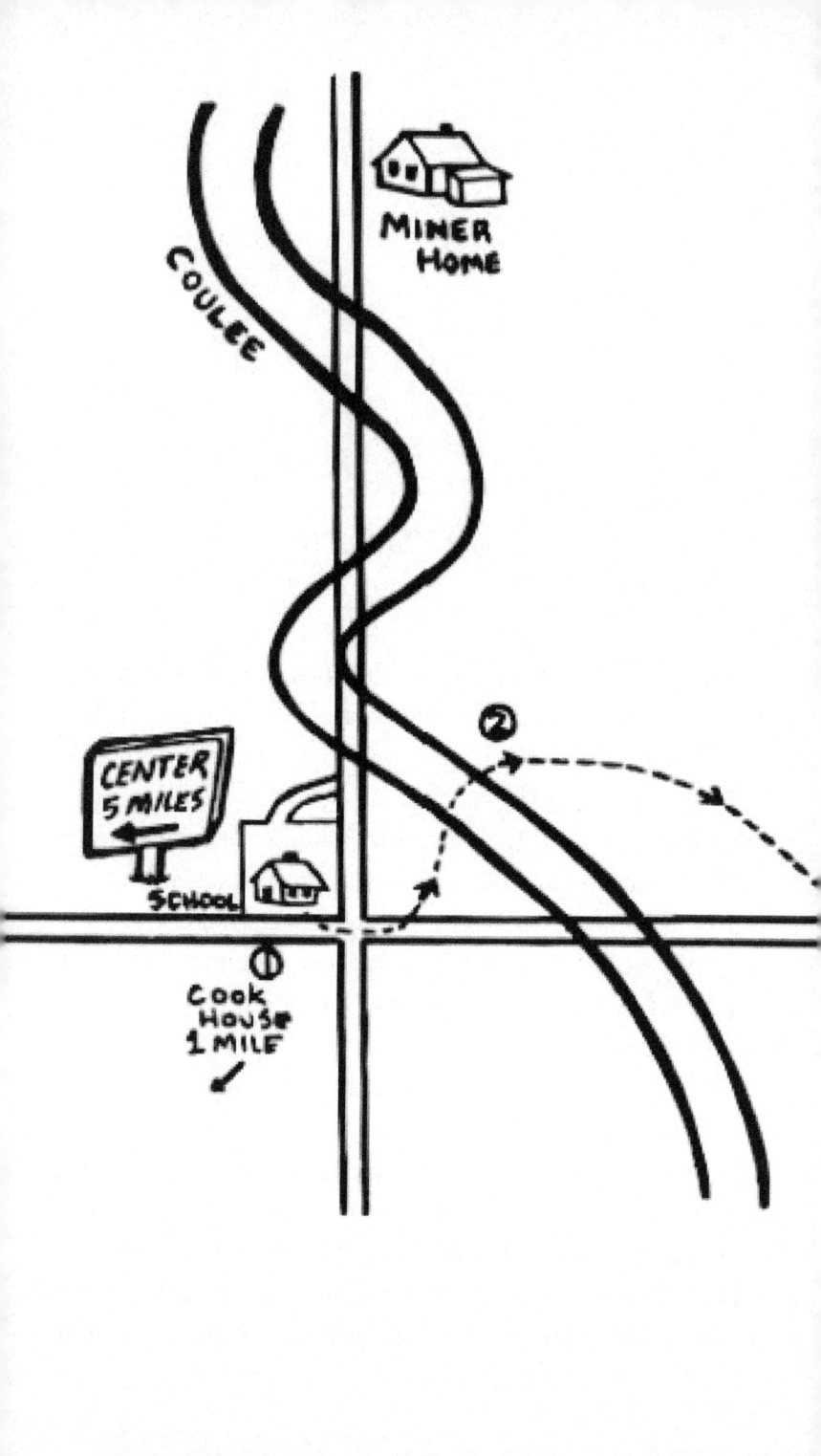

COULEE

MINER HOME

CENTER 5 MILES

SCHOOL

②

① COOK HOUSE 1 MILE

STARCK HOME

③

④ TIPPED OVER

sure wasn't that great. Heck, with cold winds gusting up to 60 miles per hour driving all that snow, it must have been almost impossible."

Grandpa looked at his two grandchildren. They were both totally into the story, even more than he had expected they would be.

He continued drawing as he was talking, "The wooden floor became their wall on the east side. Remember, the canvas top was ripped quite a bit, but it now provided at least some protection from the cold snow on the ground. The back of the overturned sleigh was open to the north, and that's where most of the wind was coming from. The front of the sleigh faced south, and it was open, too, but not much wind was coming through that end.

"So Hazel yelled to her brother and sister over the wind, 'Let's build a nice, cozy shelter! Could you two help me find the blankets and the robe?'

"They soon found them. Then Hazel spread the two blankets out on the canvas floor to provide some more protection against the cold, snow-covered ground. After that, she had Emmet and Myrdith lay down there together. Hazel told them to curl up as much as possible so they could share their body heat.

"Then Hazel hung the old fur robe up to block the north wind from getting through that north opening. Unfortunately, she couldn't find any way to secure it well enough to stop a 40 to 60 mile per hour wind from blowing it down. Also, remember the canvas had been torn before by the horses by their barn, and now the wind kept shredding it up even more. So it wasn't providing much protection at all. In a few minutes, the robe blew down and

Hazel put it up again."

"Hazel must have been *freezing*!" Thomas exclaimed. "Remember, she had been in slush up to her waist when she reconnected those tugs."

Grandpa cringed. "Poor Hazel's hands and fingers were so numb by this time," he explained, "that she struggled just to put the robe back up again. She was almost totally exhausted. But she still just kept putting the robe up every time it blew down … until she just couldn't do it anymore. By that time her hands had become so numb, she couldn't even hold onto the robe anymore."

Grandpa looked over at Kinley, and he noticed a tear was running down her cheek. Thomas was doing his best to hold back the tears.

"It was getting dark by this time," Grandpa continued, "and Hazel knew it was up to her to make the best of these impossible circumstances. So she grabbed the robe and tucked it around Emmet and Myrdith. Then she opened up her coat, held her arms out, and lay down on top of her brother and sister, holding the robe down as the wind blew relentlessly around her."

"Grandpa, what happens next?" asked Kinley. "You won't believe what Hazel did after that,"

Grandpa replied, sniffling. "I'm not sure I could have done what she did. Hazel knew no one was probably going to find them during the night in this type of weather. She knew the only way they had any chance to survive at all would be if they stayed awake all night and kept moving as much as possible. So Hazel did everything she could to make that happen.

"She told Myrdith and Emmet stories and sang any songs they knew from school and church. They said prayers. They did exercises—like Hazel had them open and close their fingers 100 times while she counted. They'd move their feet around and act like they were running. Hazel would even punch them lightly to keep them awake. She told Myrdith and Emmet to punch each other to help keep awake. "The snow was now getting into the sleigh big- time, and in a short time, it formed a heavy crust around their legs. When that happened, Hazel got up and broke it so Emmet and Myrdith could keep moving."

"I wish Hazel could have gotten under the covers, too," said Thomas.

"Emmet tried to get his big sister to get under the covers with them several times," said Grandpa, "but Hazel knew it wouldn't work. There just wasn't enough room, plus the wind would soon have blown off their blankets and the robe if Hazel wasn't holding them down. As Hazel got more and more exhausted and cold, she made her brother and sister promise that they wouldn't go to sleep, even if she did."

"Did they promise?" asked Kinley.

"Yes, they did," Grandpa replied. "And they kept that promise."

"What was happening to Old Maude all this time?" asked Thomas.

"Maude was pretty incredible," said Grandpa. "She just stood there all night, just like she knew she had to. If she would have moved at all, the sleigh would have moved too, and the kids would have had no protection from the blizzard. All during that night, the snow and ice froze Maude's eyes and nose shut. When that happened, she'd bang her head against the side of the sled to get it off.

"As the night went on, the snow drifted over the three kids. Emmet and Myrdith eventually didn't hear Hazel anymore, but they stayed awake, just like they had promised Hazel they would. They heard a dog barking during the night, too, so there must have been a farmhouse nearby. Unfortunately, there's no way they could do anything about it in that terrible blizzard."

"Grandpa," said Thomas, tears in his eyes, "I don't want you to jump ahead in the story, but I have a feeling Hazel dies."

"I won't jump ahead," said Grandpa, taking a deep breath. "I'll tell you something right now, though. From now on, whenever you think you've really got it tough, just think back to what Hazel, Emmet, and Mydith went through that night."

"And how brave Hazel was," Kinley added.

Chapter 11

"THERE WERE DEFINITELY lots of people praying for Hazel, Myrdith, and Emmet that night," said Grandpa. "They prayed that *somehow* the kids were safe somewhere out of that awful blizzard. At the Cooks' farm house, Rufus heard the strong winds whistle through the house as he was lying in bed. He wasn't sleeping at all. He kept thinking about those three being caught out on the open prairie in all this. He kept praying the phone would ring with the emergency ring, and the message would be that the Miner kids were found and they were all okay. If that didn't happen, and they had to go out searching in the morning, Rufus prayed the weather would get better so it would improve their chances of finding them.

"Eventually, Rufus gave up on sleep, and he went out and sat in a rocking chair by the fireplace. He sat there for several minutes before he realized something—it was his *birthday*. He was 20 years old! But all he hoped this birthday would bring was some good news about the Miner children. 'No matter what,' Rufus whispered to himself, 'this is *definitely* going to be a birthday I remember my whole life.'

"Orin joined Rufus at about three in the morning. The two talked about who they were going to call and ask to join them in their search.

"Mrs. Cook got up and made them some coffee and then sat down in a chair by the fire with them. 'I just can't bear thinking of those kids out there all night,' she said, sobbing.

"'If anyone can get through something like this, it would be Hazel,' Rufus said, knowing how hard it would be to survive a night out in blizzard conditions.

"An hour before sunrise, Orin started making phone calls to many of his neighbors. As Orin made the calls, Rufus wrote down the names of all those who planned to show up at the school. While he was making the phone calls, Orin learned that about 15 men from Center planned to show up at the school, too, *if* they could make it to the school in the blizzard. With this good news, Orin figured they would have about 30 men altogether to help in the search.

"As daylight came, the blizzard conditions, unfortunately, still had not improved. Rufus and Orin dressed in as many layers of clothing as they could and went out the door. I'll tell you, it was a struggle just getting out the door and into the barn! From there, they saddled up their horses and managed to make it to the school.

"Not long after they arrived at the school, the neighbors who were on the list showed up, too. About 25 minutes after

Angel of the Prairie

that, they got another pleasant surprise. A large sled pulled by a team of mules with 15 men from Center had made it to the school. They brought 100-foot rolls of clothesline rope with them, so they could tie all the searchers together. There's no way they were going to let anyone else get lost in the blizzard.

"After a brief discussion, a man named Henry Clark from Center was chosen to be the leader of the search team. After a little more discussion, they decided they would be most effective if they set out on foot, leaving the animals behind in the school barn. So, after that, they tied themselves together and they spread out, with about 15 yards between each person.

"Rufus couldn't believe it! As they got away from the school and headed north, he couldn't even see the men on each side of him much of the time. He only felt the tug of the rope on his wrists.

"They searched the land between the school and the Miners' home, going mostly against the strong north wind—"

"But the kids weren't *there*," Kinley said, sounding frustrated, totally into the story.

"If only they would have known that," said Grandpa. "And talk about exhausting work! You two can imagine what it was like searching on this open prairie in a big blizzard. The men moved slowly, whipped around by the winds, struggling ahead. They stumbled through drifts, slipped and fell on ice, then got up again. They moved ahead with strong determination, hoping they would see *some* sign of the three kids and their jumper sled.

"By the middle of the morning, Rufus and his fellow

searchers were totally exhausted. Then word came down the line that they were going to stop at the Miner farm to see if any news had come in by phone from other searchers out on the prairie.

"When they got to the Miners, they got a chance to warm up and drink some hot coffee. A few of the neighbor women had stayed with Blanche all night, trying to help comfort her while she was waiting. Rufus would never forget the look on Blanche's face when he saw her. She had apparently sat on her rocking chair all through the night, just waiting for some news to come—but it never did.

"As the men drank the coffee, shook the snow from their coats and caps, and warmed their freezing hands by the fire, Mrs. Miner spoke to them. She told them, 'You will not find them soon enough to save Hazel. I dozed off and Hazel came to me in a dream and said, *Don't worry, Momma. I was cold, but I'm all right now.*

"Before Rufus walked out of the house to continue the search with the others, he felt more determined than ever. He hoped Mrs. Miner's words would prove not to be true. Somehow, he would help find all three Miner children—and they would *all* be okay.

"After they left the farm, they decided to work their way south again, but on a path more to the east this time. It was much easier going this time, too, because the wind was at their backs. Also, Rufus noticed the wind was going down a little. By noon, the ropes weren't even needed anymore, so they could spread out even more. Other neighbors were able to head out on horses, sleighs, and bobsleds to help with the search.

"About a mile-and-a-half east and half a mile north of

Angel of the Prairie

the school, they came to the Bill Starck farm, then they continued south. Not long after that, they struggled up a hill ... they made it to the top—then Rufus looked into the coulee in the distance. All of a sudden, he saw something move.

"Another searcher with Rufus and Orin yelled, **'That's the Miner kids' mare!'**

"A rush of adrenaline ran through Rufus's body. He ran down the ravine, lifting his knees high as he ran through the snow toward the horse, praying there would be good news. As he got closer, Maude lifted her head.

"Rufus could see the overturned sleigh, almost totally covered with snow. When he got to the sleigh, he began digging frantically. Soon, other searchers joined in the digging. ...There they were!"

Chapter 12

"RUFUS AND THE other searchers finally found them!" Kinley exclaimed, with a big look of relief on her face.

"Were they all still alive, Grandpa?" asked Thomas.

"Yes," Grandpa replied. "After removing all the snow covering them, they found Hazel first. She was still lying over her little brother and sister, with her arms still outstretched, now frozen in that position. Hazel was unconscious and she had a very slow pulse, plus she was having a lot of trouble breathing. Tears came to Rufus's eyes as he helped break the crust that had formed around her all those hours. As he helped lift her out of there, Rufus noticed the ice sheet that had formed from Hazel's waist on down."

"That's from where the sleigh got stuck in the coulee that first time, when the tugs came loose," said Thomas.

"That's right," said Grandpa. "So they quickly but tenderly covered Hazel with lots of blankets and carefully put her on a horse-drawn sleigh that was waiting nearby. It took off right away for the Starcks' farmhouse, less than a mile away.

"Then Rufus ran back and watched as several men were carefully removing the robe that covered Myrdith and Emmet. It was sort of pasted together with the snow and ice that had accumulated around the two of them the last several hours. When they finally pulled it off, they got a pleasant surprise. The two children looked up at them, dazed, but they looked to be all right."

"They're okay?" Kinley asked.

"Yes, they were," said Grandpa. "Myrdith and Emmet definitely looked stunned, but Emmet immediately asked if Hazel was okay. Rufus told them that she had just been taken to the Starck house, where they would take good care of her." "'We couldn't hear her for a long time,' Emmet managed to say to the rescuers, 'but we stayed awake all night, just like she told us to.'

"'We're going to take you two to the Starcks' house and get you nice and warm,' Rufus told his two young friends.

"The rescuers made sure Myrdith and Emmet were wrapped up in plenty of blankets. Then they tenderly put them onto another sleigh which headed for the Starck farmhouse. As Rufus got on another sled to follow, he couldn't help but notice three large haystacks less than 20 yards away. If only the Miner kids had been able to see them, the haystacks *certainly* would have provided much better shelter than the overturned sleigh did."

"That's so sad," said Thomas.

"It sure is," said Grandpa. "This next part of the story is even sadder. I'm not sure I even want to tell you about it."

"Please do, Grandpa," Kinley pleaded.

"Yeah, Grandpa," said Thomas. "Please tell us."

"Okay," said Grandpa, taking a deep breath. "When

Hazel was brought into the Starcks' home, one of the little Starck children named Anna was there. She would remember what happened and tell people about it her whole life. Anna would never forget Hazel's frozen, outstretched arms, as she was carried into the house. She would never forget the sound she heard when Hazel's frozen arms brushed against the furniture in the living room. Then Hazel was carefully carried into the parents' bedroom where several neighbors tried to help her."

"That's so sad, Grandpa," said Thomas, holding back tears.

Grandpa handed Kinley a Kleenex. She was beggining to cry.

"After that," said Grandpa, "Anna remembered a lot of crying … so much crying. … I can't even imagine all the emotions everyone in that house must have been feeling. Soon, Emmet and Myrdith arrived, and several more neighbors helped those two in another room. They were both suffering from frostbite and exposure, but otherwise, they seemed okay."

"Hazel died, didn't she?" Kinley asked, not really wanting to know the answer.

"She never regained consciousness," said Grandpa, sadly. "She died before sunset that day."

"Just like in her mother's dream," said Thomas.

"That's so sad, Grandpa," said Kinley, wiping more tears from her eyes. "Did Hazel's parents get to the Starcks' house before she died?"

"Yes, they did," said Grandpa, handing a tissue to Kinley and Thomas, who wiped tears from their eyes.

"This is really a sad story, but it's really wonderful, too," said Kinley.

"Yeah, Grandpa," Thomas agreed, tears in his eyes. "I guess not every good story can have a completely happy ending."

Chapter 13

"THE FUNERAL MUST have been really sad," said Kinley.

"Are you sure you want me to tell you about that?" asked Grandpa.

"Yes. Please do, Grandpa," said Kinley. "Please tell us," Thomas pleaded.

"All right," said Grandpa. "The funeral was on Friday the 19th of March at ten-thirty in the morning. All the businesses in the town of Center were closed for the day. By then, many people from all around that part of the state had heard about Hazel's heroism. People showed up in large numbers at the small Methodist Episcopal Church in Center to pay their last respects. The church was totally packed that morning. Rufus stood in the back of the church with Orin Cook and some other friends. It's lucky that it was pretty nice out, because several hundred people actually had to stand outside during the funeral. They opened up the small front door of the church and a window so people could hear what was going on inside." Grandpa paused and took a tissue from the Kleenex box on the kitchen table. "All the kids from the school were sitting in ront of the church," he said, wiping the tears from his eyes.

"Were Myrdith and Emmet well enough to come to the funeral?" Th omas asked.

"Yes, they were sitting with the family in front," Grandpa answered. "Th e Miner kids were all there, along with Blanche and William."

"I can't imagine how sad everyone must have been," said Kinley, who took a tissue from the box and wiped some tears from her eyes.

Methodist Episcopal Church

"That's for sure," said Grandpa, sniffling. "I would have cried as soon as I saw all those kids in front of the church. It must have been a tough funeral to get through, but Reverend Madsen was the perfect person to deliver the sermon. After all, he had been one of the searchers with Rufus and Orin, and he was in the Starck house as they were trying to revive Hazel. He had also spent a lot of time the past few days with the family. During his sermon, he did an excellent job telling the story of Hazel's amazing sacrifice. Reverend Madsen preached his sermon from John 15:13, which says, 'Greater love has no one than this, to lay down one's life for one's friends.'

"The minister also mentioned Old Maude, who had not moved during the 25 hours out in the blizzard and sacrificed her life."

"Old Maude was a hero too, wasn't she?" said Thomas, taking a Kleenex from the box.

"No doubt," Grandpa replied. "If Maude would have moved, the sleigh would have moved, and the only cover and protection the kids had, would have been gone. Poor William Miner was also mentioned by Reverend Madsen during the funeral sermon. William had spent most of those awful 25 hours by himself, wading through the coulee, hoping to find his kids."

By this time Grandpa, Thomas, and Kinley were all using their Kleenex.

"At the end of the funeral," Grandpa said, "six of the friends and classmates of Hazel helped pick up the casket, and they carried it slowly to the hearse, out in front of the church. By this time, there wasn't a dry eye anywhere inside or outside the church."

Angel of the Prairie

Grandpa cleared his throat. "After that, everyone went to the cemetery, within walking distance of town. Rufus walked there, and he would never forget seeing Hazel's parents as they said good-bye to Hazel for the last time, as the other Miner children stood nearby.

Grandpa, Kinley, and Thomas didn't say anything for the next several seconds.

"Grandpa, I loved that story," Thomas said, breaking the silence, "even though it was really sad."

"I think that's my new favorite story," said Kinley. "Everyone should know about this wonderful story."

"I agree," said Grandpa. "Most of the stuff I found about it came from old newspaper clippings and talking to old-timers around Center. Someone should really write a book about it."

Kinley's whole face lit up, and she looked at Grandpa. "Maybe the three of us could write a book!" she said excitedly. "You've given us a great start, Grandpa!"

"That's a great idea!" said Thomas. "Could we, Grandpa?" "If you two want to give it a try, I'd love to work on that with you," said Grandpa.

"That's awesome, Grandpa!" exclaimed Kinley.

"You're the best, Grandpa!" said Thomas.

Kinley asked, "Grandpa, do you think we could get some flowers and put them by Hazel's gravestone sometime?"

"If we're going to be writing a book together," said Grandpa, "we might be spending quite a bit of time in Center. We will definitely make sure we take some flowers to Hazel's gravesite."

Chapter 14

KINLEY AND THOMAS couldn't wait for summer to arrive. Finally, they would have time to write a Hazel Miner book with their grandpa.

On the first Saturday in June, Grandpa came over to Bismarck and picked up Thomas and Kinley for a trip to Center. On the way, they stopped for breakfast at Ohm's Cafe on the west end of Main Street in Mandan.

Grandpa loved Ohm's. He had been eating there since he was a little boy. He used to stop there on the way home from his little league baseball games and buy a white, licorice Popsicle or an ice cream bar. In high school, he always stopped there for burgers and fries on the way home from football games with his friends.

Grandpa used to tell Kinley and Thomas about the *good old days* when his parents could pick up ten hamburgers and a large bag full of fries there on Wednesday nights, all for just two dollars. It fed their whole big family with eight kids.

While they were eating breakfast at Ohm's, Kinley asked, "Grandpa, do you know what happened to Emmet,

Myrdith, and Rufus after the blizzard and everything?"

"I know a little bit," said Grandpa as he reached for his billfold, opened it up, and took out a folded piece of paper. "That's something I thought maybe you could help me find more information about, now that you're out of school for the summer," he said, as he unfolded the piece of paper and looked at it. "This is what I found out so far. I'll start with Emmet. He was the easiest to find something about. Some of my friends actually knew Emmet and his family. You see, Emmet and his wife, Mamie, actually lived in Bismarck. It turns out Emmet painted houses."

"Did he have any children?" Thomas asked.

"Yes, three," Grandpa answered, looking down at his piece of paper. "Two girls and one boy. Their names were Lorraine, Mary Kay, and Gene."

"What about Myrdith?" Kinley wanted to know.

"I found out she got married to a guy named Ralph Casady," said Grandpa. "They had one child, a boy named William."

"Named after Myrdith's dad?" Kinley guessed.

"Yes," Grandpa answered.

"Do you know where they lived?" Thomas asked.

"A small town named Selah, out in Washington State, just north of Yakima, but that's really all I know about Myrdith so far."

"It's going to be a fun challenge trying to find more information," said Kinley.

"Did you find out anything about Rufus?" asked Thomas.

"Well, this was really exciting for me," Grandpa said, smiling. "Last week, I actually talked to Rufus's daughter,

Lona, for about two hours on the phone. It turned out Rufus lived in Hot Springs, South Dakota, much of his life with his wife, Jeannette. That's where Lona lives now. Rufus and Jeannette had three kids —two boys named Dawn and Blaine, and, of course, one girl named Lona."

"Did you say one of the boys was named *Dawn*?" said Kinley.

"That's right," said Grandpa chuckling. "Lona told me that Dawn wasn't too thrilled about that name his whole life. Apparently, Jeannette had read a story about an Indian boy with that name, and she picked it for that reason."

"That's pretty funny," said Thomas.

"You're not going to believe this," said Grandpa. "I found out more good stuff from Lona. We already know Rufus had his twentieth birthday on the day that Hazel Miner and the kids were found, March 16, 1920. Well, Lona told me that Rufus died at the age of 83 on March 18, 1983."

Thomas's eyes got bigger as he looked at Grandpa. "March 18—that was just two days after his birthday and *your* birthday and two days after Hazel, Myrdith, and Emmet were found."

"And, if Rufus would have lived one more day," Kinley noted, "it would have been exactly 63 years after Hazel's funeral."

"You two are way too smart!" said Grandpa with a big smile.

Thomas asked, "Did you find out what Rufus did to make a living, Grandpa?"

"He pretty much remained a cowboy his whole life," Grandpa answered. "He worked on other people's ranches and eventually on a ranch of his own. Lona told me that he was known to be a great horse rider. He also got his horse to do some pretty cool tricks. I actually have a photo on my phone that Lona sent me of Rufus with his trick horse, Red. Lona told me the photo was taken when she was just a little girl."

Grandpa showed the photo to Kinley and Thomas. "That is so cool!" said Kinley.

"I can't believe you actually got this from Rufus's daughter!" said Th omas.

"I have a feeling we will make more exciting discoveries as we're writing this book," said Grandpa.

Kinley asked, "Did Lona tell you whether Rufus ever talked about Hazel, Emmet, and Myrdith?"

"Yes," Grandpa replied. "He talked about them a lot, especially on his birthday each year. She said Rufus often had dreams about the morning they found the three Miner children. In his dreams, when they found Hazel with her arms frozen and still outstretched, something really wonderful happened. Hazel suddenly turned into an angel, and she talked to Rufus."

"What did Hazel say to him?" asked Kinley.

"Hazel told Rufus she was very happy in heaven, and he shouldn't ever worry about her. She also told Rufus she was sorry his birthday didn't work out the way it was supposed to." "Grandpa!" Kinley said excitedly. "I think I have the perfect title for our book! How about *Angel of the Prairie!?*"

"I love it!" Thomas exclaimed.

"Me too!" said Grandpa. "I don't think there could be a better title, Kinley!"

Chapter 15

WHAT AN EXCITING time Grandpa, Kinley, and Thomas had that day! The three of them took turns taking photos of many of the important places in the Hazel Miner story.

Chapter 16

GRANDPA, KINLEY, AND Thomas walked toward Grandpa's truck after they visited Hazel's monument. Grandpa looked at his watch and said, "It's time we get to the cemetery. There's a little surprise waiting for you two there."

As soon as they got there, Kinley took the bouquet of flowers out of the cooler and they walked to Hazel's gravesite. When they got there, they were met by a man holding a guitar.

Grandpa said, "Kinley and Thomas, this is a friend of mine, Chuck Suchy. Chuck and I went to school together at Mandan High School many years ago. Chuck, these are my two grandchildren who plan to write a book about Hazel Miner with a little of my help."

"That's fantastic!" said Chuck, with a big smile. "Your grandpa didn't tell you, but I've written a song about Hazel Miner, and he wanted me to sing it to you this afternoon. It's called 'The Story of Hazel Miner.'"

Chuck Suchy sang Hazel's song. It brought tears to the eyes of Grandpa, Kinley, and Thomas.

Angel of the Prairie

Wings on snow, a fate not chose,
Morning finds a dove so froze,
Who too soon thought the spring arrived,
In warmth below, her love survived.

Up in Oliver County, on the West Dakota plain,
Lived a farmer's daughter, Hazel Miner was her name.
She was soon to come in bloom, a prairie rose of spring,
She'd never see the young-girl dreams her sixteenth year
would bring.

Hush a bye, don't you cry, cold is like sorrow,
Sing a song, it won't be long, you'll be warm tomorrow.

A 1920 mid-March storm caused school to let out early,
So each child could reach their farm before the blizzard's fury.
With her brother, sister, bundled tight, Hazel hitched the
sleigh, But in the night of blinding white, she somehow lost
her way.

For half a day they plodded on, then darkness, desperation,
Hazel put the young ones down, and laid her body o'er them.
Through the night she gave them songs and stories to sustain,
Near the dawn, her strength all gone, three by sleep were
claimed.

Hush a bye, don't you cry, cold is like sorrow,
Sing a song, it won't be long, you'll be warm tomorrow.

Silent song, paling wind, storm at end, again begin.
Not all to soar the winds aloft, stiffened wings, feathers soft.

The next day the searchers came, found the horse still standin'
Its eyes and nose frozen closed, no duty more demandin'.
They lifted Hazel from the snow, only limp her hair.
With sadness, joy, the girl and boy, alive beneath her there.

Hush a bye, don't you cry, cold is like sorrow,

Kevin Kremer

Sing a song, it won't be long, you'll be warm tomorrow.

Wings on snow, a fate not chose,
Morning finds a dove so froze,

Who too soon thought the spring arrived,
In warmth below, her love survived.

Hush a bye, don't you cry, cold is like sorrow,
Sing a song, it won't be long, you'll be warm tomorrow.
Hush a bye, don't you cry, you'll be warm tomorrow.

"That was awesome!" Thomas said when Chuck was finished.

"That was so beautiful," said Kinley, wiping tears from her eyes. "I believe Hazel is up in heaven … and she just heard you singing her song … and she loved it."

"What inspired you to write the song?" asked Thomas. Chuck explained, "Actually, way back in the 1980s, my daughter Andra, who was nine years old at the time, read an article in the paper about Hazel Miner. When she was done, she handed it to me and told me to read it. I was fascinated by the story, and I actually went to the State Library in Bismarck to do some more research on it after that. Then I wrote the song."

"Well, it's wonderful!" Grandpa exclaimed.

"I still think about Hazel all the time," said Chuck, "especially when I hit a bump in the road in my life and wonder what I should do. Hazel did the best she could do, and good came from her efforts, even though she died in the process."

"Do you think we could put the lyrics from your song in our book?" asked Kinley.

"I'd be honored," said Chuck. "I'd also love to have a copy of your book that's signed by all three authors when you're finished."

"Oh, I think that can be arranged," said Grandpa.

Kinley walked over, bent down, and put the flowers on Hazel's gravesite. She whispered, "I love you and your story,

The Miner Home Site: Howard Bieber, who now lives on the Miner farm, points to where the Miner home once stood. The home was made of cottonwood logs, it was in poor condition, and was torn down in the 1970s.

Angel of the Prairie

The school: Center Consolidated School, now a home, looks like this now. Th e classroom for the upper grades was on the left; the classroom for the lower grades was on the right.

The back of the old school.

Kevin Kremer

The old flag pole, still standing at the school.

The old swing at the school, still looking good enough to swing on.

Angel of the Prairie

The front of the Starck home as it looks today. It is now owned by Clay Starck, grandson of Bill Starck from the story. Clay's dad was a five-year-old boy living in the house in 1920.

The back of the Starck home.

Kevin Kremer

The old school barn behind the trees. The barn is now at the Starck farm. In 1960 or 1961, Clay Starck's dad bought it from the school board, tore it down, and reassembled it on the Starck farm, using it as a granary. It's now used for storae.

The school bar

Angel of the Prairie

Inside the old school barn.

This is believed by many to be the first coulee in the story, where the horse and jumper sleigh got stuck, and Hazel got soaked helping get them out.

The second coulee, where the jumper sleigh tipped over.

The museum and the Hazel Miner Monument at the Oliver County Courthouse in Center, North Dakota.

Angel of the Prairie

The Hazel Miner Monument: There was talk about building a hospital to honor Hazel, but Hazel's parents said that they preferred a monument of some kind. School children from all over North Dakota and beyond collected money for the monument. A former North Dakota governor named L.B. Hanna and his family loved the Hazel Miner story, and they made sure the monument was put up in 1936.

Kevin Kremer

ABOUT THE AUTHOR:

Dr. Kevin Kremer has written more than a dozen children's books, and he particularly enjoys writing books about real people. He has already written books about George Armstrong Custer and Teddy Roosevelt. This book about Hazel Miner is his third book of historical fiction.

Kremer also likes helping other authors with challenges they are having with their own book projects. He has helped dozens of people write books ranging from children's picture books and chapter books to adult fiction and nonfiction.

Dr. Kremer has started a writing-publishing company to help people with book projects of any kind. To contact him regarding book or e-book projects, school author visits, or to purchase books, go to:

Web site: KevinKremerBooks.com
E-mail: snowinsarasota@aol.com
Phone: 941-822-0549

ABOUT THE ARTIST:

Dave Ely was once a student in author Kevin Kremer's sixth grade class in Bismarck, North Dakota. Now, Dave is Kremer's favorite artist.

Dave is a self-taught artist with many talents. Besides illustrating books, he does custom wood carvings, bone sculptures, and paintings. Many of his works depict a Western or wildlife theme.

Ely has done a life-sized bear carving, an eagle carving forthe movie *Wooly Boys*, and a life-sized carving of a mountainlion. He presently works at the Dakota Zoo in Bismarck, North Dakota.

Dave loves to get away from it all by camping and fishing. Red Lodge, Montana, is his favorite spot.

To view some of Dave's work or to contact him, go to: **www.elywoodcarving.com.**

CHILDREN'S BOOKS

A Kremer Christmas Miracle

The Blizzard of the Millennium

Spaceship Over North Dakota

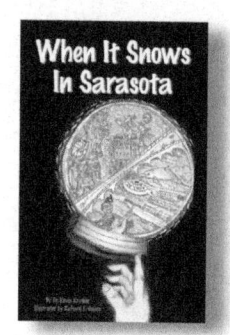

When It Snows In Sarasota

Saved By Custer's Ghost

Santa's Our Substitute Teacher

BY KEVIN KREMER

Are You Smarter Than A Flying Gator?

The Most Amazing Halloween Ever

Maggie's Christmas Miracle

Are You Smarter Than A Flying Teddy?

The Year Our Teacher Won The Super Bowl

To arrange for a reasonably priced author visit or to buy other great books, go to:
KevinKremerBooks.com

Published by Kremer Publishing 2019
P.O. Box 1385
Osprey, FL 34229-1385
941-822-0549

Made in the USA
Middletown, DE
16 March 2020